HOUSEHOLD

Publications International, Ltd.

Contributing Illustrators:
Lane Gregory, Jeff Moores, Terry Presnall, Bot Roda

Louis Weber, CEO
Publications International, Ltd.
7373 North Cicero Avenue
Lincolnwood, Illinois 60712

ISBN-13: 978-1-4127-1498-3
ISBN-10: 1-4127-1498-2

Manufactured in China.

8 7 6 5 4 3 2 1

CONTENTS

SIMPLE SOLUTIONS FOR HOUSEHOLD HEADACHES

Are you stymied by stubborn mineral deposits on your shower doors? Frustrated by too little storage space? Defeated by ants soldiering across your kitchen counters? No matter how fastidious and organized you are, maintaining your household is bound to present you with an array of challenges.

Household Secrets has an abundance of practical and clever solutions for both major and minor household headaches. And it's filled with tricks that simplify everyday tasks.

Chapters are devoted to cleaning, organizing and storing, laundry and clothes care, decorating, safety and security, and pest control. Each offers simple and effective tips and strategies that will help you keep your house in tip-top shape with a minimal amount of time and effort. *Household Secrets* even includes recipes for powerful natural household cleaners and stain removers that are easy on your budget.

From the attic to the basement and the living room to the garage, you can count on *Household Secrets* to help beautify, organize, protect, and clean your home and everything in it.

CLEANING

There are plenty of
cleaning products out
there, but buying and
trying them all would
cost you dearly in
both money and time.
And you might still
end up with that
nasty rusty ring
around your bathtub
drain or that fine layer of grease coating your plastic
storage containers. What you really need, instead,
are the secrets to effective, efficient, and affordable
household cleaning. You'll find those secrets,
collected room by room, in this chapter.

BATHROOM

The bathroom gets dirtier more quickly than any other
room, except perhaps the kitchen. How yucky it gets

will be determined, at least in
part, by the number of people
who are using it and how dili-
gent they are about cleaning up
after themselves. Fortunately,
most bathrooms are made of
materials that are easy to clean.

Clean the bathroom at least once a week. The following tips can help ensure that you spend as little time and elbow grease as possible keeping this all-important room comfortably clean.

Shower Stall

Even if you wipe them down after every use, shower enclosures are a chore to keep clean—but they can be less of a problem if you follow these suggestions for preventive care and maintenance:

- Leave the shower door slightly open after showering to allow air to circulate. This will discourage mildew growth.

- Help prevent mildew from taking hold by wiping shower walls with a towel after each shower.

Shower Stall Cleaner

1 cup vinegar

½ teaspoon dishwashing liquid

¼ cup dishwasher rinse agent

Mix ingredients together. Apply to shower walls with a sponge. Rinse well and wipe dry.

- Remove hard-water deposits on shower enclosures with a solution of white vinegar and water.

- Glass shower doors will sparkle when you clean them with a sponge dipped in white vinegar.

- Add 1 cup fabric softener to 1 quart warm water, and use to loosen and clean soap scum from shower doors. Or wipe the doors with a fabric softener sheet to remove the scum.

- Showerheads can get clogged with mineral deposits from your water, reducing water flow. Remove deposits by mixing ½ cup vinegar and 1 quart water in a large bowl or bucket. Remove the showerhead and soak it in the vinegar solution for 15 minutes. For plastic showerheads, soak for 1 hour in a mixture of 1 pint vinegar and 1 pint hot water. Brush deposits loose with an old toothbrush. Clean the holes by poking them with a wire, pin, toothpick, or ice pick.

- If you have a clogged showerhead that is too stubborn to come apart, make a soaking bag for it by filling a resealable plastic bag with white vinegar. Wrap the filled bag around the showerhead and attach it with a rubber band. Keep it wrapped overnight, and by morning the head should come loose. (Even if it doesn't, any mineral deposits that have been clogging the showerhead should be dissolved.)

- Mix 1 part mineral oil with 4 parts water in a clean, empty spray bottle. Spray mixture on soap scum in your shower or tub, then wipe clean with a sponge.

- Remove water spots on metal frames around shower doors with lemon oil.

- When tile walls need a thorough cleaning, run the shower water at its hottest temperature so the steam will loosen the dirt. Then, using a sponge mop, clean with a mixture of ½ cup vinegar, 1 cup clear ammonia, and ¼ cup baking soda in 1 gallon of warm water. After cleaning, rinse with clear water. Never use harsh abrasive powders or steel wool pads.

- Fiberglass shower and tub surrounds need special care because fiberglass scratches easily. Clean these areas periodically by spraying them with vinegar and wiping with a sponge. Never use abrasive cleaners; instead, try baking soda and a sponge dampened with vinegar.

- Coat the tile walls of your shower with furniture polish to prevent soap scum buildup and water spots.

Shower Curtain & Bath Mat

Like shower stalls, shower curtains are subject to the mildew monster. But they're easy to clean if you follow these secret strategies:

- Keep a new shower curtain looking fresh by using the old shower curtain as a liner. Hang the new curtain on the same hooks in front of the old curtain. The old curtain will take the beating from water and soap scum while the new one stays clean.

- Eliminate mildew by spraying newly washed shower curtains and rubber or vinyl bath mats with a disinfectant.

- Keep vinegar in a spray bottle near the shower, and squirt shower curtains once or twice a week to fight off soap film and mildew. No need to rinse.

- Sometimes mildew will leave a stain on shower curtains if not promptly removed. To remove these stains, mix borax with enough vinegar to make a paste, then use it to scrub the stained area.

- Clean a rubber or vinyl bath mat by tossing it into the washer with some bath towels. The terry cloth scrubs the mat, and everything comes out clean.

Bathtub

Bathtubs are gunk collectors, trapping everything from soap scum and hair to rust and mildew. How you clean your tub will depend on what it's made of. Porcelain tubs can stand up to stronger products than those made of fiberglass and acrylic. Regular cleaning makes the task much easier!

- A ring around the bathtub can be rubbed away without cleaners by using a nylon net ball or pad.

- Cover a stubborn bathtub ring with a paste made from cream of tartar and hydrogen peroxide. After the paste dries, wipe it off.

- Discolored porcelain fixtures can be cleaned with a tartar-hydrogen peroxide paste or with a paste made of borax moistened with lemon juice. Scrub the paste into lightly stained areas with a brush, and rinse well.

- Powdered automatic dishwasher detergent makes a great ring remover. Sprinkle some on the rings and wipe with a wet sponge—or sprinkle some on a wet sponge and wipe.

- Soak paper towels with undiluted vinegar and place them on the ring. Let towels dry out, then spray with straight vinegar and scrub with a sponge.

Sink

Sinks are easier to clean than tubs, and these tips will help keep them looking more like new.

- Whiten yellowed porcelain sinks and tubs by treating them with a paste of salt and turpentine. Wearing rubber gloves, apply the mixture with a stiff brush, let sit for 15 minutes, then wipe with a damp sponge and rinse thoroughly.

- Brighten porcelain fixtures with club soda. Spray or drip the soda onto the fixtures and rub with a soft cloth to shine.

- Hard-water and mineral deposits around sink and tub faucets can be removed by covering stained areas with paper towels soaked in vinegar. Leave towels on for 1 hour, then remove and wipe with a damp sponge.

- Plug the sink drain, then pour in ½ cup vinegar and fill the sink with water. Let sit for 1 hour, then scrub any mineral deposits with an old toothbrush. Rinse.

Drains (Bath & Kitchen)

- Clear a slow drain by pouring ½ cup baking soda followed by ½ cup vinegar down the drain. (*Caution: The interaction of these two ingredients creates foaming and fumes; replace the drain cover loosely to prevent them from escaping.*) Flush the drain with clear hot water after about 3 hours.

- Mix together equal parts vinegar, salt, and baking soda, and pour the solution down the drain. Let it sit 1 hour, then pour boiling, or very hot, tap water down the drain.

- Pour a strong salt solution (1 cup salt and 2 cups hot water) down the kitchen drain to eliminate drain odors and break up grease deposits.

- A sink clog made up of greasy foods may be dislodged with ½ cup salt and ½ cup baking soda. Sprinkle this solution into the drain, then flush with hot tap water.

Toilet

Cleaning the toilet may not be your favorite task, but it's one that will keep your bathroom looking and smelling fresh. The following tips will make the job a snap. One caveat first: Never mix chlorine bleach with ammonia or vinegar, as they can create toxic fumes when combined.

- Pour vinegar into toilet and let sit 30 minutes. Next, sprinkle baking soda on a toilet bowl brush and scour any remaining stained areas. Flush.

- Once a week, pour 2 cups vinegar into toilet and let sit. (Tip: Rest toilet bowl brush inside bowl with lid closed to remind yourself and family members not to use the toilet until it gets brushed!) After 8 hours or more, brush toilet well and flush. This regular treatment will keep hard-water stains at bay and clean and freshen your bowl between major cleanings.

- Use powdered laundry detergent combined with baking soda for a homemade toilet bowl cleaner. Just mix 1 cup baking soda with 1 cup detergent. Each time you clean, sprinkle ¼ cup of this mixture into the toilet and let it sit for 10 minutes. Scrub briefly, then let sit another 10 minutes. Brush again, then flush. When stubborn stains are a problem, drop detergent directly onto the stain and scrub.

- Clean and disinfect with ½ cup bleach. Pour it into the bowl, and let it stand for 10 minutes. Scrub with a toilet brush, then flush.

- Give your toilet an overnight cleaning by putting ¼ cup borax in the bowl and letting it sit overnight. In the morning, scrub the stains away.

- You can achieve the same effect as above by putting two denture cleanser tablets in the toilet bowl and letting them sit overnight. Follow up with a little scrubbing in the morning.

KITCHEN

Cooking is a messy task, but daily cleanups can help keep things under control. Some kitchen cleaning jobs, though, are bigger ones that you'll undertake less frequently. Here are some ways to get them done fast.

Refrigerator

Are you in the habit of opening and closing your refrigerator door quickly so you don't have to see what's growing inside? Even if you're pretty good about cleaning up spills and wayward food particles, the refrigerator will still harbor icky stuff that you need to attend to—especially waaaay back.

- To clean and refresh the inside of your refrigerator, sprinkle equal amounts of salt and baking soda on a damp sponge, then wipe refrigerator surfaces.

- Deodorize the inside of your refrigerator by wiping it down with a sponge soaked in vanilla extract. To help deodorize it even more, soak a cotton ball in vanilla extract and leave it on a saucer in the refrigerator overnight.

- Make your refrigerator shelves easier to wipe down and keep clean by coating them with paste wax.

- Prevent mildew buildup inside your refrigerator or on its rubber seals by wiping occasionally with a sponge dampened in undiluted vinegar. No need to rinse afterward.

Substitute Tools

- An automobile snow brush is perfect for cleaning under the refrigerator.
- Use an old shaving brush or baby's hairbrush to avoid harming delicate fabric or pleated lamp shades when dusting.
- Paintbrushes make excellent dusters for small or hard-to-reach areas. Flick them along doorjambs, around windows, and into corners where dust cloths won't fit.
- Instead of buying dust cloths chemically treated to "attract" dust, make your own from cheesecloth. Dip the cloth in a solution of 2 cups water and 1/4 cup lemon oil, and allow to dry before using.
- An old nylon stocking rolled into a ball becomes a nonscratch scrub pad for cleaning the sink and tub.
- Dust and other debris often collect behind large appliances. Clean out these hard-to-reach areas by making a yardstick "duster." Here's how: Just cover the end of a yardstick with an old sock (thick cotton ones are best), and secure it in place with rubber bands, or fasten a small sponge to the end of a yardstick using staples or rubber bands.

- To clean sticky refrigerator door gaskets, mix 4 tablespoons baking soda with 1 quart water, and apply the solution with a toothbrush. Wipe clean. This also helps control mildew buildup.

- Fill a small bowl with instant coffee crystals and place it on the back of a shelf in your refrigerator or freezer to control odor buildup.

Clean Cleaning Supplies

Revitalize old, smelly sponges by soaking them for 10 minutes in a bleach and water solution. Mix ¾ cup bleach with 1 gallon water. Be sure to rinse them thoroughly afterward.

Dishwasher

Even though the purpose of dishwashers is to clean what's inside of them, they are also prone to mineral buildup, mildew, odors, and stains. Here's how to take care of these longer-term problems.

- Clean out hard-water stains while deodorizing the dishwasher—leaving it sparkling—by running it empty using powdered lemonade mix instead of detergent. The ascorbic acid in the powder provides the cleaning action.

- If the interior of your dishwasher retains odors, sprinkle 3 tablespoons baking soda in the bottom of the machine and let it sit overnight. The odors will be washed away with the baking soda during the next wash cycle.

- Remove hard-water stains from the inside of the dishwasher by loading it with glassware and china and putting ¾ cup household bleach in a bowl on the bottom. Run a complete wash cycle, then put 1 cup vinegar in a glass bowl and place the bowl in the dishwasher. Run another complete wash cycle.

- To clean smudges from the exterior and to remove stains from the liner, dip a cloth into baking soda and rub.

- Add ½ cup vinegar to an empty dishwasher and run the rinse cycle. This will open up any clogs in the dishwasher drain lines and deodorize the machine.

Microwave

Even if you're really careful, food has a tendency to pop or explode when being heated in the microwave. The intensity of the excited molecules can pop a lid right off a container. That means the ceiling and walls of your microwave will likely need vigilant upkeep and an occasional all-over cleaning.

- If your microwave is spattered with old sauces and greasy buildup, mix 1 cup water with ¼ cup vinegar in a glass measuring cup and put it inside. Boil for 3 minutes, then remove measuring cup and wipe inside of oven with a damp sponge.

- Use a mild dishwashing detergent, baking soda, or glass cleaner to clean the inside of the microwave. Wash the glass tray in the sink or the dishwasher if it's soiled.

- Deodorize your microwave by keeping a dish of vinegar inside it overnight. If smells continue, change vinegar and repeat nightly until the odor is gone.

Homemade Countertop Cleaner

½ cup vinegar

⅓ cup ammonia

2 teaspoons baking soda

1 gallon hot water

Mix together all the ingredients and apply the solution with a sponge. Rinse with clear water and buff. Use this cleaner on acrylic, ceramic tile, cultured marble, and plastic laminate countertops. Dirt and soap film are quickly and inexpensively removed with this mixture.

Caution: Wear rubber gloves and work in a well-ventilated area when using this powerful solution.

Stove Top

Your stove top is like a drop cloth, displaying all your recent culinary adventures in the form of spatters, spots, and spills. Using a spoon rest and and splatter guard will cut down on the mess, as will dealing with whatever falls on the stove top sooner rather than later.

- Use club soda to clean your stove top. Just pour it directly on a sponge and wipe. Rinse with warm water, then dry thoroughly.

- Use a fabric softener sheet to wipe away grease splatters.

- Clean up any spill on your stove top more easily by sprinkling it with salt first. The mildly abrasive quality of salt removes stuck-on food, but it won't mar the stove top's surface.

- Clean burned-on food from a stove-top burner by sprinkling it with a mixture of salt and cinnamon, then wiping away immediately. The mixture will give off a pleasant smell and cover up any burnt odor the next time you turn on the burner.

- You can also use a mixture of salt and cinnamon to soak up a liquid spill on a stove-top burner. Sprinkle the mixture on and leave it for

5 minutes. After it has absorbed the excess liquid, wipe it away.

- Spray a painted or wallpapered wall behind your stove with furniture polish, and buff it with a soft cloth. This prevents any grease splatters from sticking to the wall.

- Mix 1 tablespoon dishwashing liquid with ½ cup household ammonia and enough water to fill a spray bottle. Use this mixture to cut grease and clean the stove top—or any greasy surface. Store the cleaning solution for future use; just be sure to label the bottle.

Oven

There's nothing quite as scary as the prospect of cleaning the oven's cavity. It's serious work! But here are some tips to make oven cleaning speedy and successful.

- Get rid of stubborn baked-on blackened food by "steaming" it off with ammonia vapors. Lay the racks on old towels in your bathtub. Fill the tub with warm water and ½ cup ammonia. Let the racks sit in the water for ½ hour. Be sure the bathroom is well ventilated. Rinse.

- When cleaning your oven, finish by wiping the entire surface with a sponge dampened with a mixture of equal parts white vinegar and water. This will help prevent greasy buildup.

- If a pie or similar sugary item boils over onto the oven floor, sprinkle the sticky spill with salt. Let it sit until the spilled area becomes crisp, then lift off with a spatula when the oven cools.

Homemade Oven Cleaner

Pour 1 cup ammonia into a glass or ceramic bowl, place it in a cold oven, and allow it to sit in the closed oven overnight. The next morning, pour the ammonia into a pail of warm water and use this solution and a sponge to wipe away the loosened soil. *Caution: Wear rubber gloves whenever you work with an ammonia solution. The fumes are strong at first, but they soon dissipate.*

Range Hood

These useful appliances are positioned to take the brunt of cooking grease and soil. Here's how to degunk them.

- Twice a year, "de-grease" the vents of your oven hood. Wipe them with a sponge and undiluted vinegar, or remove the vents and soak them for 15 minutes in a mixture of 1 cup vinegar and 3 cups water.

- Wipe the exterior and the interior of the range hood regularly. When you need to give it a thorough scrub, use a solution of hot water, dishwashing detergent, and ammonia to cut the grease. Wear rubber gloves when working with ammonia.

Garbage Disposal

Considering what goes down them, it's no wonder that disposals sometimes reek. But you can make yours smell great in a jiffy.

- Remove odors from your garbage disposal by pouring bleach down the drain. Then run hot water for 2 minutes.

- Citrus peels are another great odor eliminator. Tear up and throw peels into the disposal, then grind them with a stream of cold running water.

- Baking soda can deodorize disposals, too. Sprinkle baking soda over ice cubes and grind them in the disposal.

- Households with septic tanks should deodorize the garbage disposal with ½ cup baking soda and 1 cup vinegar. Let sit 20 minutes, then briefly run hot water.

FLOORS

You can eliminate some of the dirt that gets tracked into the house by asking people to take off their shoes at the entryway. But floors will still get dirty. How you clean what lies beneath your feet depends on what it's made of. We have tips for all kinds of flooring.

Ceramic Tile

- To make your floors sparkle, mop them with a combination of 1 cup vinegar and 1 gallon warm water.

- For heavy-duty cleaning, mix ¼ cup low-sudsing, all-purpose cleaner, 1 cup ammonia, and ½ gallon cool or cold water. Apply the solution to the floor with a sponge mop, using pressure for heavily soiled areas. Rinse with cool, clear water for spotless results. Dry with a soft cloth. Caution: Wear rubber gloves, and

Homemade Floor Cleaner

  1 part white vinegar

  1 part rubbing alcohol

  1 part water

  3 drops dishwashing liquid

Combine all ingredients and use mixture to clean the entire floor. Or keep it in a spray bottle for spot cleaning and deodorizing. This solution is good for laminate and tile floors.

work in a well-ventilated area when using this powerful solution. (This solution can also be used on asphalt, concrete, flagstone, and slate floors.)

Linoleum & Vinyl

- Scrub a linoleum floor with a mixture of 1 gallon water and 1 cup vinegar. If floor needs a polish afterward, use straight club soda.

- To quickly clean up a spill, dip a sponge in dishwashing detergent and wipe.

- Remove black scuff marks with toothpaste. Rub the paste into the mark and wipe away with a damp cloth. To enhance the scrubbing power, add a little baking soda to the toothpaste.

- Mop up salt deposits from winter boots with an equal mixture of vinegar and water.

- When damp mopping, add 1 cup fabric softener to ½ pail water to keep the floor shining.

- Spray furniture polish on your broom to help keep dust and dirt from flying away when you sweep.

Wood

- Add 1 cup plain vinegar to a gallon bucket of water, and mop lightly onto hardwood floors (do not saturate). No need to rinse. This will keep floors shiny and remove any greasy buildup.

- Closets with bare wood floors can become stale-smelling. To freshen them, lightly mop with a mixture of 1 cup baking soda and ½ cup vinegar in 1 gallon warm water.

Carpeting

- Add baking soda to the bag in your vacuum to fight odors.

- Mix 1 cup borax with 2 cups cornmeal. Sprinkle this on a smelly carpet. Wait 1 hour, then vacuum. Keep borax away from children and pets.

- Blot up a fresh coffee spill with a baby wipe, which is absorbent and nongreasy, so it won't add to the stain.

Carpet Cleaner

¼ cup dishwashing liquid

1 cup lukewarm water

This mixture is good for basic cleaning of nongreasy stains. Combine the dishwashing liquid and water, then blot onto the stain until it is gone. Rinse well and blot with a paper towel until dry.

- To remove a red wine stain, pour a bit of club soda on it. Let it soak a few minutes, then wipe up with a sponge.

- To remove tar and other stubborn sticky stuff from carpet fibers, rub vegetable oil into the substance. Rub the substance loose, then blot up the oil with a paper towel.

WINDOWS, GLASS & MIRRORS

These are all a challenge to keep clean and smudge-free. But with these tricks, your windows, glass, and mirrors will reflect well on you!

- Add 2 tablespoons vinegar to 1 cup water to make a simple and easy window cleaner. Spray the solution on windows, and wipe with paper towels.

Homemade Glass Cleaner

    2 tablespoons ammonia

    ½ cup rubbing alcohol

    ¼ teaspoon dishwashing liquid

Add all ingredients to a spray bottle, then fill the bottle with water and shake well. You can substitute 3 tablespoons vinegar or lemon juice for the ammonia. Use as you would any commercial window cleaner.

- You've undoubtedly heard that newspapers make good window cleaners. Just pour vinegar into a shallow container, then crumple some newspaper and dip it in. Wipe window clean, then use a dry newspaper for the final wipe.

- Coffee filters, of any size, can be used to polish windows or other glass surfaces. They are absorbent, lint-free, handy, and inexpensive.

- To clean the crystals on a chandelier, in a drinking glass mix together ¼ cup rubbing alcohol and ¾ cup water. Cover the floor or table under the chandelier with newspaper or plastic, and set up a ladder so you can reach the pendants. Submerge the crystals in the glass for a few seconds, swishing them back and forth. Then let them air dry.

FURNISHINGS

Every home contains a mix of materials, from brass to wood, that require different types of cleaners. We've collected tips on most of them here.

Wood Furniture

- Clean oak or mahogany furniture by wiping it with warm beer on a soft cloth.

- Cool brewed tea can be used to polish varnished wood furniture. Soak a clean cloth in the tea, wring out until just damp, then wipe.

- To remove white rings or spots, apply mayonnaise to them. Let the mayo sit for 1 hour, then wipe off with a soft cloth and polish.

- Use petroleum jelly to remove white or dark rings left on wood furniture by damp glasses. Rub the area with the jelly, let sit for 24 hours, then wipe with a clean cotton cloth.

- When a hot dish has marred the surface of a wood table, get rid of the mark with a thin paste made of salad oil and salt. Just wipe on paste, then buff slightly as you wipe off with a soft cloth.

Homemade Furniture Polish

¼ cup fresh or bottled lemon juice

½ cup vegetable oil

Mix the two ingredients in a glass jar with a tight-fitting lid. Apply to wood furniture with a cotton cloth, rubbing in a small amount at a time. This mixture can be stored for several months in a plastic or glass jar, kept out of direct sunlight.

Piano

- Remove stubborn stains from ivory or plastic keys with a cloth dipped in baking soda, being careful not to let the soda fall between the keys. Wipe the keys with another cloth and buff.

- To whiten ivory keys that have turned yellow, rub them with a soft white cloth that has been dampened with a little white vinegar. Do not saturate.

Vinyl Furniture

- Remove spots on vinyl furniture by wiping them with a cloth dipped in straight white vinegar.

- Clean vinyl upholstery with baking soda on a cloth, followed by a light washing with dishwashing liquid.

Wicker Furniture

- Keep white wicker furniture from yellowing by scrubbing it with a stiff brush moistened with salt water. Scrub, then let piece dry in full sunlight.

Metals

Brass and Copper. To clean and shine copper or brass surfaces, make a paste out of equal parts salt, flour, and vinegar. Rub on with a soft cloth, let sit about 1 hour, then wipe off and buff with a clean, soft cloth.

Chrome. Chrome fixtures, such as oven handles or mirror frames, can be cleaned of spots by simply wiping with plain vinegar. If heavily soiled, wipe with a sponge dampened with vinegar and a little baking soda.

Copper. Mix 2 tablespoons vinegar and 1 tablespoon salt to make a copper cleaner. Wash, rinse, and dry the item after this treatment. A cut lemon dipped in salt will also clean copper.

Gold. Mix 1 teaspoon ash (or baking soda) with enough water to form a paste. Rub the paste on the surface of the gold with a soft cloth, rinse, and buff with a chamois.

Pewter. Clean pewter with the outer leaves from a head of cabbage. Rub a leaf over the surface, and then buff it with a soft cloth.

You can make a safe but mildly abrasive paste to clean pewter. Add flour to a mixture of 1 teaspoon salt and 1 cup vinegar until you have a smooth paste. Apply the paste to the pewter piece, and allow it to dry for 30 minutes. Then rinse with warm water. Polish with a soft cloth, being careful to remove paste residue from all grooves or hidden areas.

Silver. Make a paste of 3 parts baking soda to 1 part water. Using a soft cloth, rub the paste gently on the silver. Tarnish will disappear rapidly. After rinsing, buff the silver with a soft cloth.

An easy way to remove tarnish from a silver piece is to place it in a glass dish with a piece of aluminum foil. Cover the silver piece and foil with 1 quart hot water mixed with 1 tablespoon baking soda. Don't use this process on raised designs, however, or you will lose the dark accents of the pattern.

One more tarnish-removal method is to mix powdered white chalk with just enough ammonia to moisten it. Rub the paste gently on the silver with a soft cloth. Rinse and buff to bring up the shine.

WALLS, WALLCOVERINGS & WOODWORK

Walls stay cleaner than most other home surfaces, but they still need your attention to look their best.

Walls

Don't judge the cleanliness of your walls by how they look. Chances are, unless you've recently cleaned them, they could use a good wash. And regular cleaning will extend the life of your paint.

- Mix together 1 gallon water, 1 cup ammonia, ½ cup vinegar, and ¼ cup baking soda in a large bucket. Stir thoroughly, then wash the walls from top to bottom, using a clean sponge and rinsing often. Wear rubber gloves to protect your hands. Stir mixture occasionally during use. Ventilate each room as you work to avoid breathing ammonia fumes. This solution can also be used to clean wood window and door frames.

- Remove crayon marks from a painted wall by rubbing them carefully with a cloth or sponge dampened with mineral spirits or lighter fluid. Remove any shine by sponging lightly with hot water.

- Clean dirty fingerprints off walls and door frames with this homemade cleaner: In a spray bottle, mix together 1 teaspoon baking soda, 1 teaspoon borax, 2 teaspoons lemon juice or white vinegar, 3 teaspoons dishwashing liquid, and 2 cups hot water. (Make sure to label the bottle to alert other household members.) Shake well before each use. Spray on trouble areas about once a week.

Wallcoverings

- To clean vinyl wallcoverings, mix together ½ cup vinegar and 1 quart water, and apply gently to the surface with a sponge. Caution: Wear rubber gloves and don't use too much solution, as it could seep under the seams and loosen the backing.

- Mix ¼ cup dishwashing liquid with 1 cup warm water in a mixing bowl, and beat the mixture to a stiff foam with an eggbeater. Working in a small area, dip a sponge into the foam and apply it to the  vinyl wallcovering to loosen dirt. Rinse the detergent with a sponge dipped in clear water and squeezed dry.

- Take a grease spot off wallpaper by first blotting it with a paper towel, then sprinkling it with cornstarch. Gently rub off the cornstarch, then vacuum the area using the upholstery brush.

Woodwork

- Cool brewed tea is an excellent woodwork cleaner. Just dip a clean, soft cloth in the tea and wipe the wood surface.

- Wipe painted woodwork clean with a mixture of 2 tablespoons dishwashing liquid and 1 gallon warm water.

- Rub mayonnaise into white water marks on wood paneling. Leave the mayo on the marks overnight, then wipe clean.

ORGANIZING & STORING

Whether you're a neat freak or a clutter king or queen, there are some principles of organization that will help you make more efficient use of available space. The first principle—which will be hard for pack rats—is the  one-year rule: If you haven't worn or used something during the past year, store it in the basement or attic. If it continues to gather dust, give it away or discard it. And be ruthless about old clothes and books (especially paperbacks) that you don't intend to read again. They'll go to much better use if donated to a charity or library book sale.

BATHROOM

If you're lucky, you may have one of those fabulous master baths that are as big as a boardroom. Most of us, though, have more cramped spaces that are a challenge to organize.

- Erect some shelves in the space beside the vanity, behind the door, or over the toilet. These will provide convenient storage without intruding on floor space.

- Install over-the-door towel racks, or place hooks on the inside of the bathroom door to hold towels and bathrobes.

- Hang a wicker basket on the bathroom wall for storing towels, tissues, soap, bath toys, and essential sundries.

- Enlist your shower rod for double duty. Attach extra shower curtain hooks to hold a back brush or a net bag for bath toys or washcloths.

- Keep toothbrushes handy but neatly out of the way on cup hooks attached to a wall or under a cabinet.

- Use an extra slot in a toothbrush holder to keep a medicine spoon handy.

- Nail files, cuticle scissors, nail clippers, tweezers, and other small metal objects are hard to store and can get lost in the medicine cabinet. Glue small magnets on the walls of the cabinet to hold them neatly and keep them from getting misplaced.

BEDROOM

The bedroom is often a catchall, so organization and sufficient storage are crucial to keep the room from being overrun.

- Use flat roll-out bins for under-the-bed storage. They can hold bed linens, sewing supplies, and infrequently used items.

- Add more storage space by building—or buying—a headboard storage unit. You can place books, lamps, or a radio on top of the unit and store extra linens and blankets on the inside.

- For a double-duty ottoman, build a plywood box with a hinged cover. Paint the outside, or cover it with fabric. Add a thick cushion for comfortable sitting, and store your magazines in style. Some stores also carry ready-made storage ottomans.

- Add a miniature hammock to a corner of a child's room for off-the-floor storage of a stuffed animal collection.

Closets

A bedroom closet can be a boon to your organizational efforts in the rest of the room. A clear, well-conceived plan will help you make the most of whatever size and shape closet you have.

- Draw an exact replica of your closet, including positive and negative features. Include all dimensions.

- Assess your wardrobe and other items to see what needs to be stored. Keep in mind that you want to store like items together: all blouses in one section, for example, and all slacks in another.

- Take advantage of all your closet space. Check whether your closet can accommodate a main clothes rod high enough to allow another rod to be installed beneath it. Hang the shorter rod at least 26 inches from the floor for slacks and shirts.

- Don't overlook the closet door—if it's the kind that opens out—for storage. Typically, the inside of the door works well for belt racks, scarves,

Quick Tricks for Your Closet
- Consider adding a second shelf above the existing one. This can be a good place to store little-used, bulky items.
- Install two rows of hooks on your closet door(s). If you have children, place the lowest one low enough for a child to reach, and the other one higher up for you to use.
- Use sturdy boxes stacked on their sides to make compartmented shelf space; you can see at a glance what's stored in the boxes.

necklaces, and other articles meant to hang. An over-the-door shoe rack will help you keep shoes off the floor or open up space on the shelf that is currently used for shoeboxes. But don't hang a laundry bag here. Anything that's bulky or protrudes is going to get in the way, and it could brush against the clothes inside the closet when the door is closed (and you DO want to keep the door closed!).

- To avoid crowding, allow 1 inch of horizontal space per garment; allow 2 to 3 inches of horizontal space for each suit, sport coat, or jacket, depending on the bulk of the shoulder padding. These estimates can help you calculate how much space you need for your wardrobe.

- Determine what needs to be hung on hangers, hung from hooks, or stored on shelves or in baskets. Everything should be allotted rod space, shelf space, or space on a specialty rack.

- The best way to utilize space is to divide it into smaller segments that closely resemble the size and shape of the items they hold. This eliminates the unruly stacks and piles of garments and accessories that are so common in closets.

- Acrylic shelf dividers provide an adaptable and easy way to segregate a shelf into specifically assigned storage compartments. These dividers are perfect for handbags, sweaters, and hats.

- Avoid using a belt ring—your belts will get jumbled. Use a belt rack that provides an ample number of hooks for the placement of individual belts and that can be installed on the side or back wall of your closet. There are also hanging belt racks that hang like a hanger on your closet's rod.

Unusual Storage Solutions

- To prevent mildew from forming in a leather-lined purse during storage, fill the purse with crumpled newspaper and leave it unfastened.
- Keep angora sweaters, gloves, and scarves from shedding by storing them in the refrigerator between wearings.
- For an instant jewelry box, line a small drawer with foam rubber. The foam will keep items from slipping around.
- Use cardboard tubing from gift wrap or paper towels to keep boots upright and in shape during nonwinter months. Or stuff boots with newspaper so they maintain their correct shape.

KITCHEN

An efficient kitchen saves both time and steps. Think of your kitchen workspace as a triangle in which the distances between the stove, refrigerator, and sink should be between 4 and 9 feet. Shorter distances mean you are too cramped, while longer distances mean you must take too many tiring steps.

- Store dinnerware and cutlery near the dishwasher so that it can be emptied quickly and easily.

- Hang placemats on a clipboard that's hung from a hook inside a cabinet or pantry door. That way, they'll stay flat and be out of the way.

- To make the most of available cabinet space when storing tapered glassware, position every other glass upside down.

- If you don't have cabinet space for your pots and pans, put a small ladder (if it's wooden, paint it to match your décor) in a corner and place the pots and pans on the steps.

- To economize on drawer space, arrange wooden spoons and other utensils bouquet-style in a handsome pitcher or canister.

- Using a magnetic strip or knife rack, hang your sharp knives inside or on the side of a high cabinet to save drawer space and to keep them out of the reach of children.

- Free up counter space by putting your microwave on a shelf above the counter.

- A wall-hung canvas apron with lots of pockets makes a decorative holder for all sorts of kitchen gadgets and utensils.

- Hanging mugs on cup hooks underneath your cabinets saves shelf space.

- If you don't have anywhere to hang a memo board for notes and messages, paint part of your kitchen door with three coats of blackboard paint.

Studly Cabinets & Shelves

If your home is built with studs and drywall, you can add cabinets or shallow shelves between the studs anywhere you need them. You'll add to your storage space without taking up any extra space. That's because the cabinets or shelves can be recessed into the wall so they're flush with it. Though narrow in depth, they can be used for

- a pantry in the kitchen
- paperback shelves in bedrooms and family rooms
- a second medicine chest or hand towel and washcloth storage in the bathroom
- displaying or storing knickknacks, small toys, or stuffed animals in a child's room
- hanging long tools in the basement or garage

LAUNDRY ROOM

- Add shelves in the laundry room to hold colored plastic baskets—one color for each family member. When you take clean clothes out of the dryer, sort each person's clothes into their basket. Family members can then pick up their baskets and fold and put away their own clothes.

- Keep two large bags near the washing machine or dryer, one for items that need mending and one for items that should be discarded. Store items as you notice them in the appropriate bag until you're ready to deal with them.

OFFICE

- No shelf space in your office? Hang slatted boxes for storage of scissors, envelopes, and other supplies.

- To brighten up an office, put pencils and pens in a flowerpot and use a music stand for a magazine rack.

- Always divide drawers into distinct compartments that prevent contents from interfering with each other. You can buy various drawer dividers, but you can also design and make your own.

- Make a household inventory book in which you keep all the instructions from appliances. Use plastic sleeves to hold receipts, warranties, and even photos for insurance purposes. Pocket sleeves can hold keys.

GARAGE

The garage, like the basement, is the place you put things you don't know what to do with. And those things tend to accumulate—seems like they even spawn!

- Insert a few well-placed hooks on the garage ceiling. These can easily hold bicycles, ladders, and luggage out of the way.

- Install hooks on the walls and hang rakes, push brooms, dustpans, and snow shovels from them. It will keep these tools off the floor and separated so you can simply grab the one you need.

- A storage shelf hung from the ceiling can hold items that are used infrequently or seasonally, such as camping gear, outdoor Christmas decorations or lights, and window screens and storm doors.

- Hang shelves on the walls or use metal bookcases to store paint and gardening supplies, tools, sports equipment, and other items. Arrange the items by category.

- Use boxes, bins, jars, and other containers to store smaller items, then arrange these containers on the shelves.

- Store nails and screws in glass or plastic baby food jars.

- Use a metal garbage can to store yard tools with long handles. Hooks can also be attached to the outside of the can for hanging smaller tools. You can lift the whole can and move it to the part of the yard you're working in.

LAUNDRY & CLOTHES CARE

There's nothing that multiplies more rapidly than laundry. No matter how many loads you do, there is always more before you know it. Learning some laundering and clothes-care skills won't decrease the amount of laundry you do, but it will extend the life of your clothes and other washables!

LAUNDRY PREP

You may be tempted just to dump a basketful of unrelated, multicolored washables into the machine—but don't do it! Your laundry will come out cleaner, and the items will look their best, if you do some advance work.

Sorting

- Sort by color first, putting all the whites in one pile, the light colors and pastels in another pile, and the bright and dark colors into a third. In the bright and dark pile, separate colorfast from noncolorfast items.

- Separate each pile into smaller piles of lightly soiled, moderately soiled, and heavily soiled clothes.

- Put white and light-colored clothes with similar degrees of soil into the same pile.

- Separate white synthetics and only wash them with other white fabrics.

Stain Removal

- Treat stains right away. The longer a stain sets, the more likely it is to become permanent.

- Pretreat spots, stains, and heavily soiled items with a prewash spot-and-stain remover, a liquid detergent, a paste made from granular soap or detergent, a bar of soap, or a presoak.

- Heat can set a stain, so avoid using hot water or a high-heat dryer setting on stained items. After washing a garment, be sure all stains are completely removed before ironing the item. Heat makes some stains impossible to remove.

A Ringing Solution

Remove ring around the collar with one of these methods:

- Rub chalk into the collar; let sit for a while, then wash as usual.
- Pour shampoo along the collar and allow it to soak into the ring. Let it sit—the longer the better—then wash.
- The grease-cutting agents in liquid dishwashing detergent can help remove ring around the collar. Paint on, let sit, then launder.

- Make a soapless spot cleaner by mixing 2 cups isopropyl alcohol (70 percent) and ¾ cup white vinegar. Pour the mixture into a clean bottle, label it, and cover tightly. Blot the soiled area until dry, then apply the cleaner with a cloth or sponge. Let it stand for several minutes, then blot the area dry again. Repeat if necessary. Blot the area with plain water after using the cleaner.

- Remove grease from fabrics by applying cornstarch or by dampening the area with salt dissolved in ammonia.

- Perspiration stains can sometimes be removed from clothing that is soaked in salt water before washing. Dissolve ¼ cup salt in a tub of water, soak overnight, then wash. For older perspiration stains, soak the area in undiluted vinegar for 15 to 20 minutes, then launder as usual. Another way to remove perspiration stains is to apply a paste of baking soda and water and let it sit for a while before laundering.

- Remove ballpoint pen stains from clothing by sponging them with milk.

- Mildew spots disappear from white fabrics if rubbed with a mixture of lemon juice and salt. Place the fabric in the sun to dry before washing.

- Immediately treat blood stains by applying a paste of cornstarch and water. Let dry, then brush off. Repeat if necessary.

- For blood-stained items, try cleaning with 3-percent hydrogen peroxide. Dab on the peroxide, then blot it off. Repeat if some stain remains. (Test a hidden area first to be sure the fabric is colorfast.)

- White socks will come out cleaner if soaked in baking soda and water to help loosen dirt before washing.

- For tough stains on baby clothes, soak the items (colorfast only) in a bucket of water to which you've added ¼ cup bleach. Wait 10 minutes, then rinse in clean water; launder as usual.

- Candle wax, chewing gum, and other gooey messes are easier to remove when they are cold and hard. Hold an ice cube against these substances to freeze them. However, if the soiled item is not washable, first place the ice in a plastic bag. After the substance has solidified, it can usually be gently lifted or scraped from the surface.

- Loosen lipstick stains from clothing by rubbing petroleum jelly into the stain before laundering.

WASHING MACHINE & DRYER TRICKS

The following tips will help you get the best results from your automatic washing and drying machines.

Loading

- Resist the temptation to overload. Your clothes will suffer, and you'll decrease the life of your washing machine. Items in the machine should appear to be moving freely around.

- Loading the washer to full capacity each time

you wash will save time and energy (that doesn't mean overload!). But don't be tempted to mix dark and light clothes in one load just to fill it.

• Mix small and large items in each load for the best circulation, and distribute the load evenly around the wash basket.

Washing

• The correct water temperature and cycle depends on the kinds of fabric being washed and the amount of soil. Use a longer cycle for heavily soiled laundry.

Special Care Items

• To machine wash fragile items, put them in a pillowcase and close it with a plastic-bag tie. Wash the bundle on a gentle cycle.
• To prevent fraying, wash a foam rubber pillow in its case. Then air dry the pillow. Do not put the pillow in the dryer.
• Glycerin will keep plastic items such as shower curtains and baby pants soft and pliable. Add several ounces to the rinse water.
• Place fabric belts and other small items in a mesh bag before washing in a machine; they will be less likely to get tangled or damaged.
• Nylon fabrics can be machine washed and dried at low temperatures. Add a fabric softener to the final rinse water to reduce static cling.
• Delicate fabrics such as silk can be safely bleached using 1 part 3-percent hydrogen peroxide mixed into 8 parts water.
• If you give your panty hose an occasional bath in a mixture of ½ cup salt to 1 quart water, they'll last longer.

- Sturdy white and colorfast items: Use normal cycle, with a 10- to 12-minute wash time.

- Sturdy noncolorfast items: Use normal cycle, with a 6- to 8-minute wash time.

- Sturdy permanent-press and wash-and-wear items: Use permanent-press cycle, with a 6- to 8-minute wash time.

- Delicate fabrics and knits: Use gentle or delicate cycle, with a 4- to 6-minute wash time.

- To boost the effectiveness of detergent for heavily soiled or greasy wash loads, add 1 cup ammonia to the wash water.

- Prevent fabric colors from bleeding by adding 2 or 3 teaspoons of salt to the wash and rinse cycles.

- There won't be any soap residue on machine-washed clothing if you add a cup of white vinegar to the final rinse water.

- Adding fabric softener to the final rinse water will reduce clinging when you wear knit garments.

- A few drops of vinegar added to the rinse water will reduce static electricity in synthetic fabrics or curtains.

- When using bleach, use the hottest water possible. Hot water improves the bleach's performance.

- To preserve the absorbency of towels, diapers, and other fabrics, use fabric softener only every third time you wash them.

- Wash, dry, and iron jeans inside out if you want them to retain their color and not look faded.

- To put body back into your permanent-press clothes, dissolve powdered milk in some water and add it to the final rinse of your washing machine.

- Give sheer curtains in your home a pressed finish without the iron. Just add a packet of plain gelatin to hot water and pour into the washing machine's final rinse.

Washing Your Washing Machine

That may sound funny, but your washing machine gets dirty, too, despite the fact that it's washing things all the time. Soap scum and hard-water minerals accumulate, so you need to wash your machine occasionally. Run the machine through a warm water cycle to which you've added a gallon of distilled vinegar. To kill germs in the machine, add ½ cup mouthwash to the wash water.

- When washing linen, use hot water for white and pastel colors and warm or cool water for dark colors. Iron linen garments while they're still damp.

Drying

- When loading the dryer, shake out each article before putting it inside. This speeds up drying time and reduces wrinkling.

- Do not overload the dryer. Overloading causes wrinkles, wastes energy, and prolongs drying time.

- Remove items from the dryer as soon as it stops, and hang or fold them as soon as possible to prevent wrinkles.

- Machine-washable slipcovers will fit smoothly after laundering if they're put back on the furniture while still slightly damp. As they dry completely, they'll shrink into place.

- Be sure that cotton garments are completely dry before storing. If you put them away damp, mildew may grow and damage them.

HAND-WASHING TRICKS

Some items can't take the rough and tumble world of the washing machine and dryer—even on the gentle cycle. Here are some hand-washing tips for these fragile pieces and other items that shouldn't be machine washed.

- Hand wash leather gloves in saddle soap while they're on your hands, but don't rub them. Rinse well and remove them. If they're hard to get off after washing, run a stream of water into them. Before drying the gloves, blow into them to help reshape the fingers. When the gloves are almost dry, put them on once more, flexing the fingers to soften the leather. Then take the gloves off and dry them flat.

- When hand washing a sweater, it's best to reach under it to lift it; if you pull it out of the water, it might stretch.

- Give extra softness to hand-washed sweaters by adding a capful of cream hair rinse to the rinse water.

- If you trace around a wool sweater on a large piece of paper before hand washing, you'll have a pattern to use when reshaping the sweater for drying. Cut out and discard the paper "sweater," and use the outside frame as your guide.

- Use towels to blot excess moisture from sweaters, stockings, panties, and bras. Hang to dry only if the weight of the water won't stretch these items out of shape. Otherwise, dry them on a towel-covered flat surface.

- When hand washing silk, use a hair shampoo containing protein. The protein in the shampoo feeds the protein in the silk.

- Add a few pinches of table salt to the water when hand washing a garment that has both light and dark colors; this prevents the darker colors from running.

GENERAL CLOTHING CARE

The care label on your clothing tells you a lot. But you won't find the following tips on it!

- Before you wear a new garment that has buttons, dab the center of each button with clear nail polish to seal the threads.

- Rub zipper teeth occasionally with wax to keep the zipper working smoothly. The stub of a candle works well for this procedure.

- To quickly remove lint from a small area, wrap a piece of tape around your finger with the sticky side out. Touch or stroke the fabric, and the lint should adhere to the tape.

- Make a do-it-yourself lint remover for larger jobs by rolling up a magazine and wrapping wide adhesive tape around it with the sticky side out.

- De-wrinkle clothing in a hurry by hanging it from the shower rod and running hot water into the bathtub. The steam will remove the wrinkles.

Iron It Out

You can cut your ironing time in half by putting a piece of aluminum foil underneath your ironing board cover. The foil will reflect the heat, so you'll actually be ironing from both sides at once.

CARING FOR SHOES

These tips will help you keep your shoes looking and smelling good.

- Remove scuff marks on shoes by rubbing with a paste of baking soda and water.

- Use a light coating of spray starch on new fabric sneakers before wearing them. Dirt won't be able to become embedded in the canvas, and the shoes will always be easy to clean.

- Use lemon juice to clean and shine black or tan leathers. Apply with a soft cloth.

- To keep shoes shiny after you've polished them, spray them with hair spray.

- Use a soft cloth dipped in vinegar to shine a pair of patent-leather shoes or any patent-leather item.

- Spray furniture polish on shoes, then buff with a clean, dry cloth.

- Neaten up the frayed ends of shoelaces (and make them easier to lace) by dipping them in clear nail polish.

Tricks, Not Treats, for Smelly Feet

- If your shoes are starting to smell, sprinkle a little salt inside them and let it sit overnight. The salt helps control moisture, which contributes to odors.
- Sprinkle baking soda into shoes to cut down on odor and control moisture.
- Fill socks or panty hose legs with cat litter, especially the scented kind. Close the ends with rubber bands, and stuff them into sneakers when you're not wearing them. The litter will absorb the odor.
- Put a fabric softener sheet inside your sneakers to deodorize them.

- Use petroleum jelly to shine leather shoes. Apply with a soft cloth, wipe off the excess, and buff with a clean cloth.

- Clean the rubber on athletic shoes with baking soda sprinkled on a sponge or washcloth.

- Hand lotion can be used to shine shoes. Just put a dab of it on each shoe, rub in with your fingers, and buff.

- Clean the salt residue common on winter boots with a cloth dipped in a solution of 1 cup water and 1 tablespoon vinegar. This will work on leather and vinyl.

DECORATING

You don't have to break
the bank to beautify your
home. This chapter will arm
you with the decorating know-
how and design fundamentals
you need to turn your place into a
palace—even on a shoestring budget.

USING COLOR

Color is the most important consideration in your decorating scheme. The colors you choose determine the
mood of the room and influence every other design
decision. Here are some pointers to help you use color
wisely and get the look you want.

- In general, the most livable color schemes use a
  light color in the largest amount, a medium
  color in the next largest amount, and the
  brightest, most intense or dark color in the
  smallest amount (as an accent).

Painting Tip

Light-colored paints dry lighter, and dark-colored
paints dry darker. That's why it's important to buy only
a small amount of your chosen color and test it on
your wall first before making a commitment to gallons.

- A long narrow room will look wider if you use a slightly darker color on the shorter walls and a lighter color on the longer walls.

- The floor should be darker than the walls to "anchor" the room. If the floor is lighter, it may appear to be floating.

- Turn a bookcase, fireplace, or piece of furniture into the focal point of a room by painting the wall behind it a darker or bolder color than the rest of the room.

- Don't choose a striped wallpaper that has a lot of contrast in the colors. Yellow and black stripes, for instance, will tend to "vibrate."

- Bring home paint chip samples and look at them in various kinds of light.

- Color is much more intense on the walls than it appears on a 1-inch paint chip. Choose a lighter shade of a color you like or have the paint mixed to produce a lighter color.

- If you're in doubt about a color, buy a quart of paint and paint one wall. Wait until it dries, then look at it in various lights to make sure it's the color you want.

- To draw attention to the ceiling, particularly if it has decorative moldings, use a colored border at the top of the walls—or use a more strongly patterned wallpaper at the top than you do lower down.

- Color can saturate your eyes. When mixing paint, look away at a white surface for several minutes to allow your eyes to adjust. You will then be able to judge the color accurately.

- Pay attention to textures when using wallpaper. Shiny surfaces, such as foils, reflect light and tend to "cool" a room; heavier textures, such as burlap and grass cloth, absorb light and "warm" a room.

TROMPE L'OEIL (TRICK THE EYE)

You can't change a room's dimensions without major remodeling, but you can fool the eye into thinking a small room is larger—or a big room is smaller and cozier—with a few tricks of the trade.

Tricks to "Enlarge" a Small Room

- Paint an oversized piece of furniture the same color as the walls.

- Install mirrors on one wall to reflect the rest of the room.

- Hang a mural-pattern wallpaper.

- Don't choose a large-pattern wallpaper. It will make the available space seem crowded.

- Small patterns with spacious, light backgrounds open up a room.

- To make a low ceiling appear higher, paper it with a small print or texture.

- The smaller the room, the more important it is to have a consistent color scheme.

- Horizontal stripes make walls look wider; vertical stripes visually raise the typical 8-foot ceiling.

- Light colors reflect light and make a space or an object look larger and airier.

- Use light-colored countertops in small bathrooms or kitchens.

- Using the same or similar colors across surfaces allows the eye to keep moving and unifies a space, making the whole area look larger.

- Floor tiles laid diagonally will make the floor appear larger than those laid parallel to the walls.

- Paint the window frames, door-frames, and ceiling the same color as the wall.

- Place furniture at angles instead of against the wall. The eye will follow the diagonal, which is longer than the wall, and the room will appear larger as a result.

- In a small bathroom, use glass shower doors rather than opaque ones or a shower curtain.

- Use a glass-topped coffee table, rather than one with a solid top, to give a more open feel to a small living room or family room.

Tricks to "Shrink" a Large Room

- Choose wallpaper with a large, bold pattern.

- To make a high ceiling seem lower, paper it with a bold pattern.

- Paint the walls a dark color. They will absorb light and make a room look smaller and denser.

- Contrasting colors stop the eye, breaking up space and making it look smaller.

- Paint woodwork and doorframes a contrasting color to the walls or leave the woodwork natural. This draws attention to the windows and doors and makes the room look smaller.

- Use bright colors for a cozier effect.

KID-FRIENDLY DÉCOR

Kids' rooms are all about color and storage. Here are some tips for both.

- Avoid heavy, elaborate window treatments that attract dust. Choose simple, washable curtains or shades. Room-darkening shades may be helpful for reluctant nappers.

- Coordinating bookcases in several sizes can give an integrated look to storage on walls of different heights.

- For a splash of color, make a variety of throw pillows and floor cushions in your child's favorite solid colors and in interesting patterns. Embellish them with juvenile trim and buttons. If you don't sew, just lay a pillow form in the center of a large fabric square, then bring the opposite (diagonal) corners of the fabric together and knot them.

Shed Some Light

If your basement stairs aren't carpeted, you can make them safer and more visible by edging them with a luminous paint.

- Instead of purchasing expensive art, stretch an interesting piece of fabric over a wood frame and hang it on a wall. Make it as big or small as you like.

- Create additional storage space with fabric skirts. Glue one side of a hook and loop fastener around the edge of a table and the other side around the top edge of a piece of fabric. When you put the two together, you have a clever skirt that hides whatever you store underneath the table. You can do the same with a sturdy box. By skirting the sides and painting the top to match the fabric, you can make an attractive end table or nightstand in no time.

- Choose two or three hues your child likes and stick with them (including shades and tints of the chosen colors, too) throughout the room. Kids' everyday clutter will introduce enough other colors and patterns, so corralling your scheme will create a calm base.

- To keep bookcases from overwhelming the space, consider painting them a pale tint to match the walls.

- If you have awkward alcoves and low walls in some areas, camouflage them with a small all-over-print wallpaper.

Kid-Friendly Storage Solutions

- Store your daughter's hair clips on a ribbon hanger. Make your own by folding the edge of a 1½-inch-wide grosgrain ribbon (36 inches long) over the bottom of a hanger. Staple in place. Clip hair bows to ribbon, and hang in the closet.

- Use transparent plastic containers with lids that are easy to remove so your child can see and access the contents.

- If you use cardboard boxes as containers, label the outside with a picture or photo to identify its contents.

Innovative Uses for Linens

- For a quick, easy, and inexpensive way to re-cover a chair, drape it with a twin-size sheet and tie or pin the corners to fit.
- A pretty or unusual blanket can substitute for a tablecloth.
- Mexican serapes and Indian bedspreads make colorful, inexpensive tablecloths—and they're great for picnics, too.

WINDOW COVERINGS

You can create many different effects using nontraditional items as window coverings—or by adding your own personal touch to ready-made blinds and shades.

- Hang shiny, metallic blinds, either vertically or horizontally, to help reflect summer sun attractively. This works especially well in south and west windows where you can't construct awnings.

- Decorative shades can make an attractive alternative to drapes, and they may be much cheaper.

- Make a curtain panel from a bedsheet by knotting the top corners around a bamboo pole.

- You can renovate your old removable-slat wooden blinds. Just spread the slats on newspaper—preferably outdoors—and spray them with a high-gloss paint or paint them with brush-on enamel.

- To add color to matchstick blinds, weave rows of colored ribbon through them.

- For an unusual window covering, attach wooden rings to a patchwork quilt and hang it from a wide, wooden rod. Don't use antique quilts for this purpose, though, as they can fade or otherwise be damaged by exposure to sunlight.

- If you have an Indian print bedspread that you don't use, hang it full-width across a window. Then open it diagonally across half the window and secure it with a tieback.

- A screen of hanging plants can be a great substitute for curtains. They offer some privacy while still allowing light.

Innovative Uses for Blinds

- Matchstick blinds can disguise a wall of hobby or utility shelves for a clean, unified look. They also can be used to partition off a closet or dressing area where you would like a lighter look than a door provides.

- Use roll-down window blinds to make a "door" for a doorless room. This is especially useful in a beach house.

SAFETY & SECURITY

You can have a clean, well-organized, and beautifully decorated home, but if it's not safe and secure, all that won't matter very much. Here are some simple and practical tips to protect your home and the people in it.

SAFETY TIPS

Stairs

- Don't use throw rugs at the top or bottom of a flight of stairs.

- Consider extending or replacing any handrail that doesn't go the full length of the staircase. Someone may assume that the stairs end where the handrail ends and miss the last step.

- If the outside of your house isn't well lit, paint the edges of the outside steps white so that they are easier to see in the dark—or install outdoor lighting.

Kitchen

- Keep baking soda on hand to extinguish a fire.

- If you see smoke or flames coming from your microwave, unplug it and leave the door shut to smother the fire.

- If a fire starts in your regular oven, turn off the heat and keep the door closed.

- Never spend more than 30 seconds fighting a fire, even if it is confined to a frying pan or wastebasket. Small fires can grow with frightening speed. If it can't be extinguished quickly, warn others to get out of the house and call the fire department.

Basement

- Light the basement with a two-socket fixture. If one bulb burns out, you won't be left in the dark.

- Paint window wells, walls, and ceiling white so they reflect more outside light.

- To make uncarpeted basement stairs safer, edge them in a luminous paint.

Pesticides

- Never spray insecticide near a flame, furnace, lighted stove, or pilot light.

- Never flush insecticides down the toilet, sewer, or drains.

- Follow the manufacturer's instructions for storage. Most pesticides should be tightly sealed and stored in a cool, dark place. Store them in a locked cabinet or on high shelves away from children.

Storms

- When a major storm is imminent, close shutters, board windows, or tape the inside of larger panes with an "X" along the full length of their diagonals.  Using even a light-weight material like masking tape may give the glass the extra margin of strength it needs to resist cracking.

- When a tornado threatens, move to an underground shelter, such as a basement in a home or building. If no basement is available, move to an interior room or hallway on the lowest floor. Position yourself under a sturdy piece of furniture for protection. Stay away from the windows.

- Always keep a battery-powered radio in your home so that you can tune in to radio stations and get emergency information if you lose electricity. Check or change the batteries frequently—or buy a crank-type radio that recharges batteries with a few turns of the hand crank.

- Keep a flashlight in an easily accessible spot on every floor of your home. Check the batteries monthly, and replace them as needed. Or buy  hand-crank flashlights to ensure that you always have a reliable light source.

SECURITY

- Assess your home's vulnerability by thinking like a burglar. You'll discover weaknesses that you may not have noticed before.

- Install quality window and door locks—and use them! About 30 percent of burglars gain entry via unlocked windows or doors.

- When installing a window lock, drip some solder on the screw heads. It will stop a burglar from unscrewing the lock after cutting a small hole in the windowpane.

- Make sure the outside of your home is well lit at night. Exterior lighting should allow visibility for 100 feet and illuminate front and back entrances, pathways, and garage doors.

- Replace ordinary porch lights or side-door lights on single-family homes with motion-detector lights.

- Install quality 1-inch throw deadlock bolts on all exterior doors.

- Make your house look the same whether you're home or away. Use a timer to turn on lights at the front and back of your home every day, not just when you're away. The lights should turn on in a way that mimics daily activity. This establishes a pattern that will not appear suspicious when you're gone. The same kind of timers can be used to turn on televisions and radios. There are even timer systems available to open and close curtains.

- If you're going to be away from home, adjust your telephone ringer to its lowest volume. An unanswered phone is a quick tip that your home is empty.

- Inventory and mark your belongings with an identifying number. Thieves have a harder time selling marked items. An engraving pen is the best marking device. You can borrow one without charge from your local police department. Do not use your Social Security number for identification! Instead, mark the items with your driver's license number so they can be easily traced back to you if recovered.

PEST CONTROL

Bugged by bugs? There are plenty of homemade, environmentally friendly ways to get rid of unwelcome visitors. Here are some tips for making your house a critter-free zone.

ANTS

- To keep ants away from your home, mix together 1 cup flour and 2 cups borax in a quart jar. Punch holes in the jar's lid, and sprinkle the concoction outside around the foundation of your home. Borax is toxic; keep away from children and pets.

- Put several bay leaves on clean cabinet shelves to get rid of ants and other tiny insects. This will also discourage return visits.

- Carpenter ants are attracted to damp wood, so if you see this kind of ant, check your pipes, roof, and windowsills for water leaks.

Make Ants Walk the Line

Whenever you see ants coming into your home, block their entry with a line of dried-out coffee grounds, chalk, vinegar, or all-purpose flour. Ants either don't like to or can't cross over certain substances. They may be repelled by them, or they simply may not be able to follow the lead ant after it has stepped in something.

- Sprinkle anthills liberally with talc-based baby powder. The ants will try to relocate their hill, but if you keep sprinkling it with powder, they'll get the message and move to your neighbor's yard.

COCKROACHES

- A mixture of borax and flour also helps control roaches. Just combine ½ cup borax and ¼ cup flour and sprinkle the powder along baseboards and doorsills—or spoon it into jar caps positioned under sinks or cabinets. Keep away from children and pets.

- Supermarkets and grocery stores almost always have roaches in them. When unpacking food at home, check bags and boxes to be sure you haven't brought any home with you.

- Turn cocky cockroaches into little bug statues: Mix together equal amounts of cornstarch and plaster of paris. Sprinkle around cracks and crevices in your home. When a roach feasts on the mixture, it will be "inactivated."

- Another cockroach solution: Briefly heat 1 teaspoon boric acid with 1 teaspoon corn syrup in a microwave. Stir so that the boric acid completely dissolves. Place this mixture in bottle caps around your home, or use an eyedropper to apply it to cracks. Just be sure to keep pets and children away from the solution.

RODENTS

- The scent of peppermint repels mice. To discourage rodents from entering your home, place sprigs of peppermint where they are likely to gain access. Or you can soak pieces of cardboard in oil of peppermint and leave them in appropriate places.

- If you're trying to trap a mouse, raw bacon or peanut butter makes good bait. A cotton ball saturated with bacon grease works well, too. When setting the trap, be sure the bait is placed so the mouse will have to tug at it, triggering the trap. If you're using peanut butter, dab some on the triggering device and let it harden before setting the trap. If bacon is your bait, tie it around the triggering device.

- To keep rodents out of your house, seal every opening they could squeeze through. (Some can pass through openings of less than $\frac{1}{4}$ inch.) Put poison in deep cracks or holes, and stuff them by pushing in steel wool or scouring pads with a screwdriver. Close the spaces with spackling compound mixed with steel wool fragments.

MEALWORMS

- You won't be bothered by mealworms if you place a few sticks of wrapped spearmint gum in your cabinets near open packages of spaghetti, noodles, or macaroni. Mealworms like pasta, but they are repelled by spearmint. Don't unwrap the gum—it will dry out and lose its scent.

- Store flour in the freezer to kill mealworm larvae and prevent them from hatching.

BEES & WASPS

- If a bee, wasp, or hornet is flying around your house and you don't have any insect spray, hair spray is a good substitute. (This works on other flying insects, too.)

- If bees are nesting in a wall but you don't know exactly where, tap the wall at night and listen for where the buzzing is the loudest. You may also be able to feel the heat of the hive through the wall—the nest is usually about 95 degrees Fahrenheit. Check by drilling a small hole in the area you suspect. If the drill bit comes out with honey or paraffin on it, you'll know you've located the nest.